A Special Gift

For

MY DEAR SISTER MARJ,

From

YOUR SISTER ALLISON.

Date

22 - 8 ~ 1999

Message

THANK YOU FOR EVERYTHING
GOD BLESS

Time for Reflection

HELEN STEINER RICE

TINY TREASURE-SERIES

R Fleming H. Revell

TIME FOR REFLECTION

You can't light a candle
To show others the way
Without feeling the warmth
Of that bright, little ray.

Light is shed upon the righteous
and joy on the upright in heart.

Psalm 97:11 NIV

Today remind yourself of the
radiance and illumination that
can be spread by just one
small flame.

Games can't be won
Unless they are played,
And prayers can't be answered
Unless they are prayed.

The sacrifice of the wicked is an
abomination to the Lord, but
the prayer of the upright is
his delight.

Proverbs 15:8

Today pray with a sincere heart.
Pray earnestly and constantly.

We love the sound of laughter
And the merriment of cheer,
But our hearts would lose
their tenderness
If we never shed a tear.

May those who sow in tears
reap with shouts of joy!
Psalm 126:5

Today appreciate the
importance of both laughter
and tears.

We are all God's children,
And He loves us – every one,
And completely forgives
All that we have done.

*Train up a child in the way he
should go, even when he is old
he will not depart from it.*

Proverbs 22:6 NAS

Today repeat, "God loves me
and God forgives me."

Trouble is only a challenge
To spur you on to achieve
The best that God has to offer
If you have the faith to believe!

The fear of the Lord is the
beginning of knowledge ...
Proverbs 1:7

Today, with faith in your heart,
you can face any trouble that
you encounter.

There are always two sides –
The good and the bad,
The dark and the light,
The sad and the glad.

*He who seeks the good
commands favour, but he who
pursues evil will have evil
befall him.*

Proverbs 11:27 NAB

Today keep an open mind
in all matters.

Stop wishing for things
You complain you have not,
And start making the best
Of all that you've got.

*I pour out my complaint before
him, I tell my trouble
before him.*

Psalm 142:2

Today be happy with what you
have – not discontent with what
you don't have.

Show us that in quietness
We can feel Your presence near,
Filling us with joy and peace
Throughout the coming year.

Hide your loved ones in the
shelter of your presence, safe
beneath your hand, safe from all
conspiring men.

Psalm 31:20 TLB

Today ask Jesus to share your
concerns and confidences.

Show me the way, not to
fortune or fame, not to win
laurels or praise for my name ...
But show me the way to spread
the great story
That Thine is the kingdom, the
power, and the glory.

*I have seen you in the sanctuary
and beheld your power and
your glory.*

Psalm 63:2 NIV

Today concentrate on ways to
spread the Good News.

No day is too dark
And no burden too great
That God in His love
Cannot penetrate.

Be not wise in thine own eyes:
fear the Lord, and depart
from evil.
Proverbs 3:7 KJV

Today whatever occurs,
whatever burden you shoulder,
keep steadfast in your trust
of God.

May He who hears our
every prayer
Keep you in His loving care –
And may you feel His
presence near
Each day throughout the
coming year.

*The Lord is near to the
brokenhearted, and saves the
crushed in spirit.*

Psalm 34:18

Today and every day feel God's
presence as you look for Him
in others.

Love one another
And help those in need,
Regardless of colour,
Race, church, or creed.

Hatred stirs old quarrels, but
love overlooks insults.
Proverbs 10:12 TLB

Today concentrate on helping
others and grasp each
opportunity to offer
encouragement and assistance.

Lord, don't let me falter,
Don't let me lose my way,
Don't let me cease to carry
My burden day by day.

*I relieved your shoulder of the
burden; your hands were freed
from the basket. In distress you
called, and I delivered you.*
Psalm 81:6, 7

Today, with God's help, carry
your burdens and seek solutions.

It does not take a new year
To make a brand-new start,
It only takes the deep desire
To try with all your heart.

Take away the dross from the
silver, and there comes out a
vessel for the smith.

Proverbs 25:4 NAS

Today continue to try. Focus on
asking God to help in your
decisions and not relying only
on your own strength.

In this changing world,
May God's unchanging love
Surround and bless you daily
In abundance from above.

But as for me, my prayer is to
thee, O Lord. At an acceptable
time, O God, in the abundance
of thy steadfast love
answer me.

Psalm 69:13

Today you may not understand
why you are facing adversity or
you may question God's plan,
but someday you will
understand it all.

If you meet God in the morning
And ask for guidance
when you pray,
You will never in your lifetime
Face another hopeless day.

Oh, sing to him you saints of his;
give thanks to his holy name. His
anger lasts a moment; his favour
lasts for life!
Psalm 30:4, 5 TLB

Today meet and greet the Lord
with hope in your heart.

I come not to ask, to plead,
Or implore You,
I just come to tell You
How much I adore You!

... I trust in the steadfast love of
God for ever and ever.

Psalm 52:8

Today express your love for
God in a way that is pleasing to
Him ... by living His
commandments.

Happiness is a state of mind
Within the reach of everyone
Who takes the time to be kind.

He who oppresses the poor
shows contempt for their Maker,
but whoever is kind to the
needy honours God.
Proverbs 14:31 NIV

Today take the time to befriend
a co-worker or a neighbour.
Volunteer to drive an elderly
person to a medical appointment
or cook a meal for a new mother
just home from the hospital.

God's mighty hand
Can be felt every minute,
For there is nothing on earth
That God isn't in it.

O sing to the Lord a new song,
for he has done marvelous
things! His right hand and
his holy arm have gotten
him victory.

Psalm 98:1

Today thank God for holding
you in the palm of His hand –
a hand that is both gentle
and strong.

God truly loves you
Come what may ...
He will lead you and protect you
Every step along life's way!

*O Lord, lead me in Thy
righteousness because of my
foes; make Thy way straight
before me.*

Psalm 5:8 NAS

Today, when seeking a solution
to a problem, confidently take
the most difficult step: the very
first step.

God, help me in my own small way to somehow do something each day
To show You that I love You best and that my faith will stand each test.

I kept my faith, even when I said, "I am greatly afflicted."
Psalm 116:10

Today accomplish at least one act of kindness no matter how small or insignificant it may seem.

Forgive the many errors
That I made yesterday
And let me try again, dear God,
To walk closer in Thy way.

*I acknowledged my sin unto
thee, and mine iniquity have I
not hid. I said, I will confess my
transgressions unto the Lord;
and thou forgavest the iniquity
of my sin.*

Psalm 32:5 KJV

Today make a sincere effort to
eliminate errors and those
occasions that could be
offensive to God.

Every day is a good day
To lose yourself in others,
And any time is a good time
To see mankind as brothers.

*A liberal man will be enriched,
and one who waters will himself
be watered.*

Proverbs 11:25

Today accept others as they are.
When you are friends with
others, you are also a friend
with Jesus.

Each day as it comes, brings a
chance to each one
To live to the fullest, leaving
nothing undone
That would brighten the life or
lighten the load
Of some weary traveller lost on
life's road.

*Blessed be the Lord, who daily
bears us up; God is our
salvation.*

Psalm 68:19

Today try to reflect God's
magnificence and brilliance into
someone else's life.

Don't start your day by supposin'
That trouble is just ahead.
It's better to stop supposin'
And start with a prayer instead.

But I, O Lord, cry to thee; in the morning my prayer comes before thee.

Psalm 88:13

Today start and end your day with prayer.

Cling to your standards
And fight the good fight.
Take a firm stand
For things that are right.

*Contend, O Lord, with those
who contend with me; fight
against those who fight
against me.*

Psalm 35:1 NAS

Today keep your standards
beyond reproach.

Brighten your day
And lighten your way,
Lessen your cares
With daily prayers.

O taste and see that the Lord is good! Happy is the man who takes refuge in him!

Psalm 34:8

Today pray and you'll find your day brighter and your way lighter.

Bless me, heavenly Father,
Forgive my erring ways,
Grant me strength to serve Thee,
Put purpose in my days.

The Lord is my strength and my song; he has become my salvation.

Psalm 118:14

Today serve the Lord by serving others. Avoid self-preoccupation. There are many who need the assistance that only you can offer.

Give us through the
coming year
Quietness of mind.
Teach us to be patient
And always to be kind.

I waited patiently for God to
help me; then he listened and
heard my cry.
Psalm 40:1 TLB

Today develop more patience
and value the calm that can
be yours.

If you desire to be happy
And get rid of the
misery of dread,
Just give up supposin'
the worst things
And look for the best
things instead.

*Happy is the man who finds
wisdom, and the man who gets
understanding.*

Proverbs 3:13

Today look for the good in
people, places, and happenings.

When you walk
down the street,
Life will seem twice as sweet
If you smile at the people
You happen to meet!

*... the cheerful heart has a
continual feast.*

Proverbs 15:15

Today let your wardrobe
include a bright, pleasant
expression. A ready smile
makes a fashionable accessory.

We know above the dark
clouds
That fill a stormy sky
Hope's rainbow will come
shining through
When the clouds have
drifted by.

*The light of the righteous
rejoiceth ...*
Proverbs 13:9 KJV

Today look beyond the stormy
formations and seek to discover
the silver lining.

We all have cares
and problems
We cannot solve alone,
But if we go to God in prayer,
We are never on our own.

... a wise man listens to advice.

Proverbs 12:15

Today if you feel lonely invite
Jesus to join you.

Unless we think we're better
Than the Father up above,
Let us forgive our sisters
and brothers
In understanding love.

Do not say, "I will do to him as
he has done to me; I will pay
the man back for what
he has done."

Proverbs 24:29

Today seek to forgive and
forget actual or imagined hurts
that have come your way.

Never be
Too busy to stop and recognize
The grief that lies in
another's eyes,
Too busy to offer to
help or share,
Too busy to sympathize or care.

*Do not withhold good from
those to whom it is due, when it
is in your power to do it.*

Proverbs 3:27 NAS

Today try to identify the heart-
hurt hidden in the words that
another is speaking.

Thank You, God, for the miracles
We are too blind to see,
Give us new awareness
Of our many gifts from Thee.

One man pretends to be rich, yet has nothing; another pretends to be poor, yet has great wealth.

Proverbs 13:7

Today develop an abiding sense of gratitude – an appreciation for the gifts of our Father.

Stop awhile to reminisce
And to pleasantly review
Happy little happenings
And things you used to do.

I remember the days of old, I meditate on all that thou hast done; I muse on what thy hands have wrought.

Psalm 143:5

Today be thankful for pleasant memories.

Seldom do we realize
The importance of small deeds
Or to what degree of greatness
Unnoticed kindness leads.

*He holds victory in store for the
upright, he is a shield to those
whose walk is blameless, for he
guards the course of the just and
protects the way of his
faithful ones.*

Proverbs 2:7, 8 NIV

Today in some manner, no
matter how seemingly small,
make the way smoother for at
least one person.

Don't ever sever the lifeline
That links you to
The Father in heaven
Who cares for you.

*The fear of the Lord prolongs
life, but the years of the wicked
will be short.*
Proverbs 10:27

Today seek ways to assist God
as He continues to care for you.

No day is unmeetable
If, on rising, our first thought
Is to thank God for the blessings
That His loving care has
brought.

Praise the Lord! Oh give thanks
to the Lord, for He is good;
for His loving kindness is
everlasting.

Psalm 106:1 NAS

Today reflect on God's
goodness. Appreciate His
magnanimity.

The nature of our attitude
Toward circumstantial things
Determines our acceptance
Of the problems that life brings.

*But I have calmed and quieted
my soul, like a child quieted at
its mother's breast; like a child
that is quieted is my soul.*

Psalm 131:2

Today minimize problems
instead of exaggerating them.

May we try to do better
And accomplish much more
And be kinder and wiser
Than in the day gone before.

*The beginning of wisdom is the
fear of the LORD, and
knowledge of the Holy One is
understanding.*

Proverbs 9:10 NAB

Today establish a deeper
understanding of situations
confronting you. Temper all
responses with wisdom and
kindness.

Love makes us patient,
understanding, and kind,
And we judge with our heart,
not with our mind.
For as soon as love enters the
heart's opened door,
The faults we once saw are not
there anymore.

*Better is a dinner of herbs
where love is than a fatted ox
and hatred with it.*

Proverbs 15:17

Today ask that love colour
your vision. Consequently, all
faultfinding will be
eliminated.

"Love one another
as I have loved you."
May seem impossible to do –
But if you will try to
trust and believe,
Great are the joys that you will
receive.

*The wise of heart will heed
commandments …*

Proverbs 10:8

Today identify the unloved and
the unwanted in your community
and then reach out to them with
a sign of love and concern.

God's help never fails
And how much we receive
Depends on how much
Our hearts can believe.

You prepare a table before me in
the presence of my enemies.
You anoint my head with oil; my
cup overflows.

Psalm 23:5 NIV

Today your heart and cup can
overflow.

In the generous heart of loving,
faithful friends,
God in His charity and wisdom
always sends
A sense of understanding and the
power of perception
And mixes these fine qualities
with kindness and affection.

*Let not loyalty and faithfulness
forsake you ...*
Proverbs 3:3

Express your appreciation to
those who serve in countless
ways: the bus driver, the
mailman, the schoolteacher,
the paperboy.

God's miracles
Are all around,
Within our sight
And touch and sound.

*Make a joyful noise unto God,
all ye lands: sing forth the
honour of his name: make his
praise glorious.*
Psalm 66:1, 2 KJV

Today take time to observe and
appreciate God's amazing
miracles.

God, teach me to be patient,
Teach me to go slow –
Teach me how to wait on You
When my way I do not know.

A man of quick temper acts foolishly, but a man of discretion is patient.

Proverbs 14:17

Today pursue the quality of forbearance.

Happiness is only found
In bringing it to others,
And thinking of all folks we meet
Not as strangers, but as brothers.

*... happy is he who is kind
to the poor.*
Proverbs 14:21

Today increase your generosity
and eliminate selfishness.

God in His mercy looks
down on us all,
And though what we've done is
so pitifully small,
He makes us feel welcome to
kneel down and pray
For the chance to do better as
we start a new day.

*O loving and kind God, have
mercy. Have pity upon me and
take away the awful stain of my
transgressions.*

Psalm 51:1 TLB

Today strive to do better than
yesterday.

Friendship is a golden chain,
The links are friends so dear,
And like a rare and
precious jewel,
It's treasured more each year.

*He who forgives an offence
seeks love, but he who repeats a
matter alienates a friend.*
Proverbs 17:9

Today write a letter to someone
– a letter of appreciation,
greeting, congratulations, get
well wishes, or cheer.

Just keep on smiling
Whatever betide you,
Secure in the knowledge
God is always beside you.

*The Lord is near to all who call
upon Him, to all who call upon
Him in truth.*

Psalm 145:18 NAS

Today maintain a happy
expression and a cheerful
attitude, knowing that God is
with you.

Everyone has his own
little niche
No matter how tiny or small,
For every life has a purpose
Or we wouldn't be here at all.

*The Lord has made everything
for its purpose...*
Proverbs 16:4

Today examine your talents
and, whatever they are, use them
to help someone in some way.

Be glad for the comfort
You've found in prayer.
Be glad for God's blessings,
His love and His care.

*The blessing of the Lord makes
rich, and he adds no sorrow
with it.*

Proverbs 10:22

Today can be a day of gladness.

No one sheds a teardrop
Or suffers loss in vain,
For God is always there
To turn our losses into gain.

For thou hast delivered my
soul from death, mine eyes
from tears, and my feet
from falling ...
Psalm 116:8 KJV

Today offer thanks to God for
always staying near to you.

"Love divine, all
loves excelling"
Makes my humbled heart
Your dwelling,
For without Your love divine
Total darkness would be mine.

*He who dwells in the shelter of
the Most High, who abides in
the shadow of the Almighty, will
say to the Lord, "My refuge and
my fortress; my God, in whom
I trust."*

Psalm 91:1, 2

Today thank Jesus for
illuminating your life.

Just follow God
unquestioningly
Because you love Him so,
For if you trust His judgment
There is nothing you need know.

*From heaven you pronounced
judgment, and the land feared
and was quiet – when you, O
God, rose up to judge, to save
all the afflicted of the land.*

Psalm 76:8, 9 NIV

Today face your problems as
they arise. Don't anticipate
trouble. The majority of worries
revolve around problems that
never occur.

If when you ask for something
God seems to hesitate,
Never be discouraged –
He is asking you to wait.

*May integrity and uprightness
preserve me, for I wait for thee.*
Psalm 25:21

Today wait if He asks you.

A cheerful smile, a
friendly word,
A sympathetic nod...
These are all priceless treasures
From the storehouse of our God.

*To make an apt answer is a joy
to a man, and a word in season,
how good it is!*

Proverbs 15:23

Today offer words of
encouragement to a friend,
parent, relative ... and to
yourself.

When your cross gets a little
heavy to wear
And a little bit more than you
think you can bear,
Remember how He
suffered and died
And allowed Himself
to be crucified.

*... they have pierced my hands
and feet.*

Psalm 22:16

Today if your cross seems
heavy, reflect on Jesus, His
suffering and crucifixion.

We know that life is never measured
By how many years we live,
But by the kindly things we do
And the happiness we give.

A generous man will himself be blessed, for he shares his food with the poor.

Proverbs 22:9 NIV

Today share a kindness – a telephone call, a ride, a loaf of homemade bread – with someone in need.

We awaken in the morning,
Wondering how we'll meet
the day,
Not knowing God stands ready
To help us if we pray.

*The integrity of the upright
guides them, but the
crookedness of the treacherous
destroys them.*

Proverbs 11:3

Today call upon God for His
heavenly guidance.

Trust God's all-wise wisdom
And doubt our Father never,
For in the kingdom of our Lord
There is nothing lost forever.

*He who walks with wise men
becomes wise ...*
Proverbs 13:20

Today work on eliminating
doubt and increasing trust.

To understand God's greatness
And to use His gifts each day
The soul must learn to
meet Him
In a meditative way.

*To get wisdom is better than
gold; to get understanding is to
be chosen rather than silver!*

Proverbs 16:16

Today make time to meditate
on God's Word.

There can be no crown of stars
Without a cross to bear,
And there is no salvation
Without faith and love
and prayer.

*Blessings are on the head of the
righteous ...*
Proverbs 10:6 NAS

Today with faith and love and
prayer as your companions,
press on to newer and higher
achievements.

There are many things in life
That we cannot understand,
But we must trust
God's judgment
And be guided by His hand.

*The Lord is a stronghold to him
whose way is upright ...*

Proverbs 10:29

Today let the direction of your
life be guided by God's hand.

Spring always comes with new
life and birth followed by
summer to warm the soft earth –
And what a comfort to know
there are reasons that souls, like
nature, must have their seasons.

He that goes forth weeping,
bearing the seed for sowing,
shall come home with shouts
of joy, bringing his sheaves
with him.

Psalm 126:6

Today compare the seasons of
the year with the seasons of
your soul.

Seek first His kingdom,
And you will possess
The world's greatest riches
Which is true happiness.

*Thy kingdom is an everlasting
kingdom, and thy dominion
endureth throughout all
generations.*

Psalm 145:13 KJV

Today when you write your
"must do" list put "seek God's
kingdom" at the top.

Our Father made the heavens,
The mountains and the hills,
The rivers and the oceans,
And the singing whippoorwills.

Let them praise the name of the Lord! For he commanded and they were created. And he established them for ever and ever; he fixed their bounds which cannot be passed.

Psalm 148:5, 6

Today be thankful for the beauty, the peace, and the marvel found in nature.

No hill is too high,
No mountain too tall,
For with faith in the Lord
You can conquer them all.

For God alone my soul waits in silence, for my hope is from him.
Psalm 62:5

Today repeat over and over,
"With God all things are possible."

Never complain
about your cross,
For your cross has been blest.
God made it just for you to wear
And remember,
God knows best!

*Trust in the Lord with all your
heart and lean not on your own
understanding; in all your ways
acknowledge him, and he will
make your paths straight.*

Proverbs 3:5, 6 NIV

Today accept your cross
uncomplainingly – for, after all,
it was personally created for you
by the Master Designer.

Most of the battles
Of life are won
By looking beyond the clouds
To the sun.

On the day I called, thou didst
answer me, my strength of soul
thou didst increase.

Psalm 138:3

Today look beyond the clouds
and you'll find some rays of
sunshine.

May we try
In our small way
To make new friends
From day to day.

A faithful envoy brings healing.

Proverbs 13:17 NAS

Today focus on the priceless
value of friendship.

The love of God surrounds us
Like the air we breathe
around us –
As near as a heartbeat,
as close as a prayer,
And whenever we need Him,
He'll always be there.

*The Lord is faithful in all his
words, and gracious in all
his deeds.*

Psalm 145:13

Todays each beat of your heart
will remind you that God is
with you.

Just close your eyes
And open your heart
And feel your worries
And care depart.

But my eyes are toward thee, O
Lord God; in thee I seek refuge;
leave me not defenceless!

Psalm 141:8

Today, as thoughts of God enter
your heart, your worries
will leave.

In the resurrection
That takes place in nature's sod,
Let us understand more fully
The risen Saviour, Son of God.

*Rise up, O Lord, and come and
help us. Save us by your
constant love.*

Psalm 44:26 TLB

Today marvel at the lesson
taught by nature on life, death,
resurrection ... and
remembrance of Jesus.

If we try to stand alone,
We are weak and will fall,
For God is always greatest
When we're helpless, lost,
and small.

*Listen, my son, to your
father's instruction.*

Proverbs 1:8 NIV

Today ask God to stand with
you. With God at your side you
can face all challenges.

I see the dew glisten in crystal-like splendour
While God, with a touch that is gentle and tender,
Wraps up the night and softly tucks it away
And hangs out the sun to herald a new day.

The sun shall not smite you by day, nor the moon by night.

Psalm 121:6

Today welcome the freshness of morning and the opportunities that await you with the start of a new day.

Happiness is something
We create in our mind,
It's not something you
search for
And so seldom find.

*You shall eat the fruit of the
labour of your hands; you shall
be happy, and it shall be well
with you.*

Psalm 128:2

Today be a messenger of
happiness.

God's presence is ever
beside you,
As near as the reach of
your hand.
You have but to tell Him
your troubles,
There is nothing He
won't understand.

*You will show me the path to
life, fullness of joys in your
presence, the delights at your
right hand forever.*

Psalm 16:11 NAB

Today converse with God and
also listen to Him.

The God who sends the winter
and wraps the earth in death
Will always send the springtime
with an awakening breath.

For thou hast delivered my soul
from death, yea, my feet from
falling, that I may walk before
God in the light of life.

Psalm 56:13

Today thank God for the gift of
changing seasons of nature and
the gift of new life.

God is no stranger
In a faraway place,
He's as close as the wind
That blows cross my face

*He it is who makes the clouds
rise at the end of the earth, who
makes lightnings for the rain
and brings forth the wind from
his storehouses.*

Psalm 135:7

Today be aware of the
omnipresence of God.

Friendship is a priceless gift
That can't be bought or sold,
To have an understanding friend
Is worth far more than gold.

*Faithful are the wounds of a
friend, but deceitful are the
kisses of an enemy.*
Proverbs 27:6 NAS

Today appreciate the
tremendous value of having an
understanding friend.

Every growing, living thing
That you can touch or
see at spring
Is but a message from above
To say that God is life and love.

*The earth is filled with your
love, O Lord; teach me your
decrees.*

Psalm 119:64 NIV

Today respond to God's
communication and His deep
devotion that repeats itself over
and over in the quality of
existence observed in the season
of spring.

All nature heeds the
call of spring
As God awakens everything,
And all that seemed so
dead and still
Experiences a sudden thrill.

*He turns a desert into pools of
water, a parched land into
springs of water.*
Psalm 107:35

Today answer God's call as
you thrill to the awakening of
the slumbering earth.

God, help me in my
feeble way
To somehow do something
each day
To show You that I love
You best
And that my faith will stand
each test.

Prove me, O Lord, and try me;
test my heart and my mind. For
thy steadfast love is before my
eyes, and I walk in faithfulness
to thee.

Psalm 26:2, 3

Today let your faith help you to
pass the test.

No one discovers the fullness
Or the greatness of God's love,
Unless they have waited
in the darkness
With only a light from above.

*Unto the upright there ariseth
light in darkness: he is gracious,
and full of compassion, and
righteous.*

Psalm 112:4 KJV

Today, thank God for being
your safety flashlight ... always
charged, always ready to shine,

Great is your gladness
And rich your reward
When you make life's purpose
The choice of the Lord.

The reward for humility and fear
of the Lord is riches and
honour and life.

Proverbs 22:4

Today act with humility.

Every burden borne today
And every present sorrow
Are but God's happy harbingers
Of a joyous, bright tomorrow.

*Know that wisdom is thus for
your soul; if you find it, then
there will be a future, and your
hope will not be cut off.*

Proverbs 24:14 NAS

Today cherish God's message
of hope.

May He who hears each
little prayer
Keep you safely in His care
And make the world around
you bright
As you walk daily in His light.

*Thy word is a lamp to my feet
and a light to my path.*

Psalm 119:105

Today welcome someone new
into your circle of friends. Let
God's light shine through you.